Daughter

OUR
STORY
REMEMBERED

Cindy
Koch

Hillary R Asbury

Daughter

OUR
STORY
REMEMBERED

CINDY KOCH

FIFTEEN·SEVENTEEN PUBLISHING

1517.

Daughter: Our Story Remembered

© 2018 Cindy Koch

Published by:
1517 Publishing
PO Box 54032
Irvine, CA 92619-4032

Illustrations by Hillary Asbury
Cover design by Brenton Clarke Little

Publisher's Cataloging-In-Publication Data
(Prepared by The Donohue Group, Inc.)

Names: Koch, Cindy. | Asbury, Hillary, illustrator. | Abridgement of (work): Koch, Cindy. Woman.
Title: Daughter : our story remembered / written by Cindy Koch ; illustrated by Hillary Asbury.
Description: Irvine, CA : 1517 Publishing, [2018] | An abridged and illustrated version of Woman: the forgotten story. | Interest age level: 010–013. | Summary: "Every little girl is courted by those who want to tell her who she is. She might be lucky enough to hear the pure and simple truth, but more often than not she will be told and believe a variety of things, some of which are not true. Where we come from and who we are is a biblical story and a beautiful one that the author hopes will guide young girls as they grow and struggle with their own identities."—Provided by publisher.
Identifiers: ISBN 9781945978142 (softcover) | ISBN 9781945978159 (hardcover) | ISBN 1945978155 (hardcover) | ISBN 9781948969048 (ebook)
Subjects: LCSH: Women—Religious aspects—Christianity—Juvenile literature. | Women—Identity—Religious aspects—Christianity—Juvenile literature. | Women—History—Juvenile literature. | CYAC: Women—Religious aspects—Christianity. | Women—Identity—Religious aspects—Christianity. | Women—History.
Classification: LCC BV639.W7 K632 2018 (print) | LCC BV639.W7 (ebook) | DDC 230.082—dc23

1517 Publishing is a boutique publishing house focused on producing high-quality, theological resources to fuel a new Reformation. We promote the defense of the Christian faith, the distinction between law and gospel, vocation and civil courage, and the proclamation of Christ crucified for you.

Printed in the United States of America

Chapter 1

I have something for you, my daughter.

I've been keeping it safe for years now, waiting for you to grow up. Tonight, I realize that it is time. No longer are you the little ponytailed toddler that I carried on my hip. Gone are the days when you and I spent many hours together in imaginary castles. Your beautiful art projects have disappeared from the refrigerator. Your baby dolls have been sleeping for many years now. Only memories remain of our silly games and fantastical stories. The make-believe fairy tales have faded back into the whispers of our past.

But tonight, I notice that you are stepping into the world and into a vast sea of stories about who you are and who you will be. These are no longer the tales that only live on the pages of your favorite books; these stories make you ask the question, "Who am I?" and will haunt your every decision. For any girl, identity is important. Along the way, you will eventually trust one of these many story lines. You might be lucky enough to hear the pure and simple truth, but more often than not, your ears will be filled with lies. Believing those lies can actually draw you away from who you are meant to be.

So I am giving you the gift of an ancient story. This is a story of character, a story of love and of sacrifice. It is a story of new hopes and amazing dreams. It has a happy ending that will certainly come true. When this story was passed to me, I was hypnotized by the beauty and simplicity of it. As you now begin the journey to become a woman, you will remember who you are and from where you came. This story will become your story.

Our great story doesn't begin on the day of your birth. Nor does it begin with mine. No, this beautiful tale opens long ago, before anything was made.

It was still.

Empty.

Blackness all around.

There was nothing but a voice.

The voice spoke, and light appeared. Day and night broke forth for the very first time. The voice spoke and water collected. Heavens above and earth below filled the empty space. The voice spoke and living sprouts of green pushed through fresh earth. Fruit trees and tiny flowers took root like never before. The voice created the earth, the stars, and life itself. This voice that spoke in the beginning of our story was the Word of God.

Because of the voice, bright, clear oceans sparkled, reflecting rays of the baby sun. Tiny new leaves sprinkled every young tree. A robin's small, sweet song sang instead of silence. That was the beginning of our story.

The Word of God was here before any of us were born. The Word was with God, building His brand-new world. But God had one more most-beloved creature to speak into creation. On the sixth day, God spoke a human onto His beautiful earth. He was so pleased with all of creation, God said, "It is very good." The Word sighed, now content, and so God rested.

The Word of God remembers the start of our journey— before we were. The Word of God remembers the glorious new mornings and fresh start of each flower. The Word of

God remembers the good and perfect beginning of your story. But guess what? This same voice is still speaking right now to tell you this story.

And so, my daughter, I pass this story on to you. I hope it will teach you to see the wise and foolish paths in our world and help you find your beautiful feminine place in it. There are so many voices that will tell you which way to go, who to trust, how to act. But this story, passed from our ancient sisters, will be your guide as you grow into a woman.

Listen, my daughter. You may not yet have wondered where you fit into God's lovely creation. You may have unanswered questions and many unasked questions as well. This story is powerful enough to carry you through the difficult times that you have yet to even imagine. Or you may think you have everything figured out right now. But you need this story like you need air to live. Each woman on this earth has a place in God's creation, and He has carefully and wonderfully made you to live a beautiful life. The story I pass to you is from the lips of the Creator of all things. He made the ground on which you stand. He gave you the eyes to enjoy each passing sunrise. He formed the very air you breathe even now. And He speaks this story into your heart and mind so that you will remember that you are His.

Little girl, here you will peek at the secrets of love. You will experience a heart of never-ending patience. You will begin to see yourself as more beautiful than diamonds. You will build your life on a strong foundation that will never crumble. You will hear your story and be incredibly blessed.

Now, my daughter, hear, love, and trust your great story.

Chapter 2

The air is fresh and calm. A young sun wraps the new earth in a blanket of perfect warmth. The whole creation seems to sigh calmly. A single human man called Adam is surrounded by creatures in this breathtaking garden. It is a glorious day of naming beasts and birds for the man. The Lord has brought him every animal: furry, feathery, scaly, large and small, brave and meek. The man has the honored job of naming all the creatures of God. Animals of every kind arrive, each one bowing to Adam, their caretaker. Earlier they crawled out from every corner of the green field, but now each one tiptoes into the bushes as the earth falls quiet again. Except for the slow trickle of the cool, clear stream, the first birds and beasts sleep peacefully.

Even though the newborn world is filled with animals, the Lord is not happy. God is worried because even after Adam names all the wonderful creations, none of them match God's great masterpiece of man. What could God be looking for? What kind of helper does He need? This human can do his jobs easily. The perfect world in which he lives gives him food and shelter. He can take care of the garden. He is in charge of God's animals and birds. God walks and talks with the man and takes care of his every need. Yet God is concerned because the man is "alone."

Suddenly, Adam's eyes become heavy. Velvety-soft ferns cushion his head as a wave of relaxation rushes over him. Peacefully, he falls into a deep, perfectly sound slumber. There Adam lies sleeping, alone.

The Lord had formed Adam limb by limb from the very dust where he now sleeps. Gathering clumps of clay, God molded him into a most impressive figure. Then God breathed His Word on that dry form in order to fill the man with life. Adam was gently placed in a stunning garden with life and water and plants surrounding him. But now the Lord God will create yet another new creature in a very special way—unlike any other animal He has made. The Lord gently pulls up the skin on one side of the slumbering Adam and takes the man's rib. God creates again.

This new creation does not come from the dust of the earth. This new creation does not magically fall from heaven. Taken from man, God makes a brand-new life. Adam's warm living bone is the foundation for a magnificent creature that could not yet be found on the earth. The Lord carefully builds a helper who completely matches Adam. None of the animals are able to be this special creature for Adam. This helper is unlike anything that has been formed from the dust; she is actually being sculpted from another living creation: the man. But the man sleeps on, unaware of God's gift of new life, which is born from his very side.

Finally, Adam's eyelids flutter, flooding his vision with a blinding light. Dark, light, flashes of morning stun his senses as he wakes up. As he focuses on the green meadow that cushioned his sleeping head, Adam catches a glimpse of an animal that he can't remember. She is incredibly attractive and yet so familiar. *Wait*, he thinks, *this is something totally different*. Blinking vigorously so as not to lose sight of her, the sleepy haze melts into a magnificent vision. Adam slowly stands up from his grassy bed, gasping between the lumps of emotion welling up in his throat. She moves smoothly to the man's quickened heartbeat. Adam's tears of joy blur her glorious walk as God presents to the man his long-awaited helper.

"Bone of my bone!" cries Adam. He recognizes this great work of his Creator from the first glance. The Lord has made a person who is Adam's perfect complement. "Flesh of my flesh," he whispers as she steps even closer. He touches her soft, warm cheek. His other arm cradles his own side from where she was taken.

"I will call her woman, because she has been taken from man," Adam says, gazing into those familiar eyes. His job of naming God's creatures is as glorious as ever when he gives this creature his own name. Her name, *woman*, means that she is from him, with him, and at his side. There is something special about this relationship. No other creature was created so intentionally from another. The very life that God gave Adam was the foundation for this woman. The Lord found Adam to be incomplete; his loneliness was not good. Man was not created to roam the garden by himself, nor was woman created to be alone. They were created for unity, togetherness, and God says His creation is now good.

God's gifts are poured upon Adam and Eve. They are both created in the image of God. They openly walk and talk with the Lord, and they completely do what they were created to do. Adam names and rules the creatures of the earth, and he also keeps the garden and protects God's gifts. Woman is created to have children and to be a help to her husband. Their special tasks flow easily from the hand-crafted bodies of their Creator. They were created to please God and to please one another. Together they are two, but one: a complete human. Both man and woman naturally and happily live in the gifts that they were given. God says this is certainly good.

Even more, God has a people who trust Him. Man and woman look to their Creator for answers, and they love His commands. They believe His word and praise Him for His amazing work. This is the fairy tale God has always intended for His creatures. He is happy to give them everything they need. He wants to live with them forever; no sadness or sickness or death will ever touch His beautiful people. All is good in the Garden of Eden.

Daughter, you might say that this is the first boy-meets-girl romance. All of our great love stories and fairy tales echo this simple story of creation. When we think about love, as our Creator made it for us, we find ourselves back in this beautiful Garden of Eden. It's the amazing beginning to our story.

Chapter 3

It all seems so perfect. But there is another creature who lives in the garden as well. There is a serpent who is wonderfully created alongside the sun and moon, the trees, and the birds. The serpent is fed by the gifts of God. The serpent is placed kindly under man's protection, just like every other creature. God looks at this creation and says, "It is good."

But the Evil Foe will use this good creature of God to lead the man and woman away from their Creator. This serpent becomes a deadly tool in the service of Satan. Satan enslaves this serpent to poison mankind with the venom of doubt.

Listen closely, daughter. This story is not to scare you. But it's important to realize how the crafty Evil One enters this lovely story in the garden. Satan twists God's good creation and pulls us away from His gifts. His evil task is to destroy our trust in the Maker of Heaven and Earth. The Word of God, His blessings and His promises, are attacked from the mouth of the Enemy.

> [The serpent] said to the woman, "Did God actually say, 'You shall not eat of any tree in the garden'?" (Gen. 3:1)

Did God really say . . . ? The serpent picks apart the Word of God so that the woman will doubt her Creator. He is not pushing the woman to disobey God. He is not asking her to hate her God or run away from His blessings. Rather, the serpent wants her to question God's Word. And she does: she begins to question everything.

> And the woman said to the serpent, "We may eat of the fruit of the trees in the garden, but God said, 'You shall not eat of the fruit of the tree that is in the midst of the garden, neither shall you touch it, lest you die.'" (Gen. 3:2–3)

Hmmm, the woman thinks, *what did God really say? "Don't eat of any tree?" No, He just said not that one. I wonder why not that one tree. I guess there is a chance we might die.* The woman has already begun to doubt God. She can't quite remember how Adam taught her God's command.

> The Lord God commanded the man, saying, "You may surely eat of every tree in the garden, but of the tree of the knowledge of good and evil you shall not eat, for in the day that you eat of it you shall surely die." (Gen. 2:16)

God actually said that they would surely, really die if they ate of this tree in the midst of the garden. But alone with the serpent, the woman remembers these words more "open mindedly" than God said them. A simple truth from God *might not* have terrible consequences. A Creator's command seems *maybe not* as serious as she once thought. The serpent smirks. He has her now.

> But the serpent said to the woman, "You will not surely die. For God knows that when you eat of it your eyes will be opened, and you will be like God, knowing good and evil." (Gen. 3:4–5)

Here, the serpent straight out lies to the woman! He plainly says the opposite of God's command. God said they *will* surely die. Satan says they *will not* surely die. Whom shall she believe and trust? By this time, though, the woman is already doubting the "good" gifts of God. But Satan is sneaky; he tells her that she will be like God, knowing good and evil, when she eats from the tree. Of course, she wants to be closer and more like her God! Her curiosity makes her inch closer and closer to that fruit God told her not to eat.

> So when the woman saw that the tree was good for food, and that it was a delight to the eyes, and that the tree was to be desired to make one wise, she took of its fruit and ate, and she also gave some to her husband who was with her, and he ate. (Gen. 3:6)

It's good fruit, she realizes. Why would God keep her from this good thing? It looks like it will make her happy. It seems that it will make her wise. She will probably be a better person if she tastes that fruit. Besides, the snake told her that she will not die. So the next thing she knows, she is looking, she is desiring, and she is eating.

It looks like Satan is the winner. Looking back over this story, we can see the difference between God's Word and the word that doubts. We are on the edge of our seats, yelling, "Stop, girl! Don't listen to that sneaky snake! He is telling you a lie!" We know God's Word is good. God spoke the Word and things were created. His Word is true and will do what it says. But this serpent looks as if he has won the battle by tricking the woman into believing a lie and not the Word of God.

The poor girl trusted Satan, the Father of Lies. Sometimes you may hear his evil voice more loudly than our Creator's voice. Satan wants to pull you away from the call of our loving God and fill your heart and mind with doubt. This Wicked Ruler of the earth will scream in your ear and make you confused. These words sound like Satan saying,

"God is wrong." He will try to cover your ears when you are listening for the outside Word of our loving God.

Because the woman did not believe and trust God above all things, the tree in the midst of the garden changed. The tree was given to both man and woman so that they could worship and show love to their God. They both were created to trust His Word and not eat of this tree. Woman was created to love God. She was made to love her Creator by clinging to His Word despite the serpent's lies, despite the desires of her heart, and despite her good reasons. But she did not listen to the Word of her Creator; she listened to the words of Satan and of her own heart. The God who created her to love and worship found her less than what she was created to be. She became an unloving, selfish, independent creature. And now the tree reminded her that she failed. This was not what God wanted for her.

Woman was tricked. But she was not alone in the garden. Her husband was with her, and he also ate. He tasted the fruit that now dulled her eyes. Both man and woman fell into a changed garden, a changed relationship with God, and a changed world.

Little daughter, I look around at this world that you are now slowly entering. There are so many things that you will find lurking in the shadows. I pray that God will keep you safe. I pray that you will trust God's Word until the end. I pray that you will remember the brilliance of our Creator's good creation in the garden that He made for you. Even though it is from before you were born, this is your great story.

Chapter 4

"It is very good," once said the Story Creator. Yet just a few sentences into the story, man and woman trade paradise for a lie. Man and woman choose a sad and lonely future. Man and woman now hide from God, which they never did before.

> Then the eyes of both were opened, and they knew that they were naked. And they sewed fig leaves together and made themselves loincloths. And they heard the sound of the Lord God walking in the garden in the cool of the day, and the man and his wife hid themselves from the presence of the Lord God among the trees of the garden. (Gen. 3:7–8)

Both Adam and his wife shudder in fear. They have both eaten the forbidden fruit now. The first bite was great, but the bitter aftertaste was unlike anything they had ever had. Cowering deep in the bushes, they feel sick from embarrassment and shame. Something is terribly different and dreadfully wrong. Instead of running into the arms of their Creator, all they want to do is run away—far, far away. Unexpectedly, this taste of knowledge and freedom has turned out to be very bad.

God watches the unhappy couple like a parent hiding in the shadows. The Lord God is no longer first in their hearts, souls, and minds. He created them to be His own. He created them to live in harmony with His Word. He created them in His image so that they might enjoy being the creature of a God who provided everything. Now they choose to be less.

> But the Lord God called to the man and said to him, "Where are you?" (Gen. 3:9)

But He does not just let the unhappy couple go; God finds His people in the garden—broken, ashamed, and with nothing. He searches for Adam and his wife. He discovers them shivering in the bushes.

> "Have you eaten of the tree of which I commanded you not to eat?" (Gen. 3:11)

The booming voice of God shakes the solid earth. The law of God comes crashing down on His beloved creation. What was once created good has now turned sour. Man and woman know they have failed—they knew it the minute they heard their God walking in the garden. They are ashamed when God calls out to them. Even though they have been caught, man and woman still can't admit their sin out loud.

The man blames everyone except himself. "This woman!" Adam exclaims. "This woman that *you* gave me! She did this!" But the woman is no better. When God asks her about this, she also blames another. "The serpent! He was the one who tricked me!" she says. Their failure is obvious, but neither man nor woman can take responsibility in the garden. Adam blames God for his transgression, and then he turns on his helper. Now this whole world is changed by a broken relationship between creatures and their God. This world that has knowledge from the tree of good and evil also has sin. God confronts the man, woman, and even the serpent with a now different description of His creation gone wrong.

First, God speaks to the serpent.

> "Because you have done this, cursed are you above all livestock and above all beasts of the field; on your belly you shall go, and dust you shall eat all the days of your life. I will put enmity between you and the woman and between your offspring and her offspring; he shall bruise your head, and you shall bruise his heel." (Gen. 3:14–15)

This was once a treasured creature under Adam's loving rule. The serpent was created by God to live on the earth. He was just as protected and loved as any other animal. But after this, the serpent's body is thrust on the ground. He is shamefully cursed more than the other animals. In this sad reality, he no longer loves and respects man but is now an enemy to the woman's children. The serpent no longer looks like what God created.

Next, He turns to His people.

> To the woman he said, "I will surely multiply your pain in childbearing; in pain you shall bring forth children. Your desire shall be for your husband, and he shall rule over you." (Gen. 3:16)

At first, the woman was made to be a mother. There was not a twinge of labor pain, not the slightest worry about her parenting technique, not even an anxious moment of concern for her babies. Woman was given the honor to help Adam where no other animal seemed fit. She was given life with God's man. But after this, pain and hard work will be her life. Fighting enters the loving relationship between man and wife. Woman doesn't find joy in her gift as helper; in fact, she fights against it. At the same time, man will now rule over her. Woman no longer looks like what God created.

> And to Adam [God] said, "Because you have listened to the voice of your wife and have eaten of the tree of which I commanded you, 'You shall not eat of it,' cursed is the ground because of you; in pain you shall eat of it all the days of your life; thorns and thistles it shall bring forth for you; and you shall eat the plants of the field. By the sweat of your face you shall eat bread till you return to the ground, for out of it you were taken; for you are dust, and to dust you shall return." (Gen. 3:17–19)

Before this, Adam was given everything on earth. He was the highlight of creation. Every task was joyful and fruitful. But now, his work becomes back-breakingly hard. Even though Adam knew of God's command, he listened to the voice of his wife instead of the voice of the Creator. Even the earth itself is affected; it will no longer produce the glorious fruits given in the garden. Adam's life is no longer easy nor everlasting. After disobeying, he sweats for food only until he returns to the dust of death. Adam and the earth no longer look like what God created.

Their history is our history. Their world continues to be our world. Their God is our very same God. We live with the consequences of man and woman's sin. Our work is hard. Our relationships are stressed. Our childbirth is painful. We struggle just to live day to day, only to labor into the dust of death. We even throw the good gifts of God back at Him.

But this tragic story, my love, took a beautiful turn when we weren't even watching. Even though they brought this twisted situation upon themselves, God doesn't leave the wretched creatures alone. He finds them cowering deep in the bushes. While both Adam and his wife are hiding, a voice from their loving Father calls to them.

> But the Lord God called to the man and said to him, "Where are you?" (Gen. 3:9)

He finds the man and woman in the garden and fights for the identity of His people. They are not abandoned outside of His love. God proclaims that this woman and man were created to be something special, beyond what any creature could destroy. There are consequences for the broken relationship, yes, but there is a solution to this problem. There will be a remedy to right all their wrongs. There will be a happy reunion of the Creator and His creations. God calls to them and gives them a simple, life-changing promise.

> The Lord God said to the serpent . . . "He shall bruise your head, and you shall bruise his heel." (Gen. 3:15)

God speaks the first gospel message to this shameful couple. There is good news given in the middle of their sin. God tells the evil serpent that man and woman will have a child that will dash his head to pieces. Now, the Lord was not simply speaking to a slimy beast gone bad. God revealed a much bigger reality in His now broken world: Satan will be defeated. Satan will be crushed. There will be no crafty snake in God's restored creation. Our terrible decisions cannot separate us from God and His gifts. Without the Enemy, Satan, and the consequences of sin, we are left with His garden of gifts. Even in the depths of their disobedience, God loved His creatures so much that He gave them a peek at victory. There is forgiveness right from the beginning. God gave a Word that He would reverse all that man and woman had done.

Although they didn't see the whole story yet, man and woman believed God's promise of life. They knew they had done wrong. They knew that they would have to leave the amazing garden of blessings. They knew they would walk a life of sorrow. But their story now looked forward to a promise of a renewed future.

> "The man called his wife's name Eve, because she was the mother of all living." (Gen. 3:20)

She is called Eve. *Eve* means "life." Adam's first task was to name all the creatures. Up until this point, his lovely woman did not bear a name. She was woman, taken from the side of man, flesh of his flesh. But now with the promise of God in the face of their sin, Adam names her true identity: she is the mother of all the living. She will be the mother of the first children on earth. She will be the mother of the promised Child that will bring all of them eternal life. *Eve* is a confession of love and forgiveness from the promise of God, spoken by the lips of Adam. When Adam looks at this woman, he tells their story. She brought an apple, knowledge, sin, disobedience, and death. Yet he names her Eve, and Adam speaks God's promise back to the both of them. He forgives Eve. He stands in the place of God and proclaims that they will be saved. He calls her "mother of all the living." He breathes on her the identity of God's restored woman.

The air is cooler in the garden now. The sun descends behind a withering tree. As the newly dead leaves float silently back to the dust of the earth, the shadow of God passes over His garden. Two snow-white lambs scream and then lie silent and motionless before their Creator. He gently lifts up the skins and clothes the naked shame of man and woman.

Daughter, God hides their sin and shame with this first sacrifice. Foreshadowing the Hero to come, God makes a way to cover their wrongs. God would continue to provide forgiveness and covering with temple sacrifices. Like much of the Old Testament story, this sweet chapter in the garden prepares us to see the greatest sacrifice of all, which covers the naked shame of the whole world.

> Then the Lord God said, "Behold, the man has become like one of us in knowing good and evil. Now, lest he reach out his hand and take also of the tree of life and eat, and live forever." Therefore the Lord God sent him out from the garden of Eden to work the ground from which he was taken. He drove out the man, and at the east of the Garden of Eden he placed the cherubim and a flaming sword that turned every way to guard the way to the tree of life. (Gen. 3:22–24)

So into the world they trudge. Adam looks ahead to sweat and hard work just so they will eat. How easy it was back in the garden, where God's good gifts abounded! Eve will soon be overcome with pain for her children. It only begins at childbirth and will continue through their lives. It would have been joyful bliss to have babies in the safety of God's garden. For the first time ever, there are disagreements between the man and woman. Anxiety, fear, fighting, sorrow—it will all end badly for the earth's first parents.

We have certainly lived too far away from the Garden of Eden. We can't begin to smell the sweet grass or feel the perfect sunshine on our faces. But we do have a Word from a God who has not left us alone. In the middle of their journey of fear and sadness, Adam and Eve hold tight to the promise of God. In hope, they watch every baby in anticipation of the "promised seed" who will defeat the Evil One. They speak the words of hope, life, and forgiveness to each other and their family.

Our story begins with tragedy, sacrifice, and a promise of forgiveness. The woman who was created beautifully did not listen to God at first. She did not believe that His gifts were good just as they were given. But the promise of life and forgiveness is who Eve is. The first female crafted by the fingers of God bears the name of life—restored to whom God intended her to be. Every daughter carries her name, her promise, and her identity.

You are a daughter of Eve. You were created by the Most High God. You now are walking outside of the Garden of Eden, bearing not just the pain of the changed world but also the promise of the Hero to come. You have been given hope in the One who will smash the head of the serpent. You, like the woman, have been found by God. You have been chosen to live as God intended His creations to live. This is your story—but only the beginning.

Chapter 5

Outside of the Garden of Eden, we look around and see the children of Adam and Eve everywhere. The beauty and peace of the garden is a distant memory, a fairy tale buried under years of dirt. The glory of God's creation has hardened into a lost legend over the years.

But suddenly, along the path of forgetful history, life is breathed back into our story. Just when we least expect it, a wandering boy enters the dull and dreary tale. In our ordinary everyday world, I see the Child who was promised in the garden right before my eyes.

> For at the window of my house
> > I have looked out through my lattice,
> and I have seen among the simple,
> > I have perceived among the youths,
> > a young man lacking sense,
> passing along the street near her corner,
> > taking the road to her house
> in the twilight, in the evening,
> > at the time of night and darkness.
> And behold, the woman meets him,
> > dressed as a prostitute, wily of heart.
> She is loud and wayward;

her feet do not stay at home;
now in the street, now in the market,
    and at every corner she lies in wait.
She seizes him and kisses him,
    and with bold face she says to him,
"I had to offer sacrifices,
    and today I have paid my vows;
so now I have come out to meet you,
    to seek you eagerly, and I have found you.
I have spread my couch with coverings,
    colored linens from Egyptian linen;
I have perfumed my bed with myrrh,
    aloes, and cinnamon.
Come, let us take our fill of love till morning;
    let us delight ourselves with love.
For my husband is not at home;
    he has gone on a long journey;
he took a bag of money with him;
    at full moon he will come home."

With much seductive speech she persuades him;
    with her smooth talk she compels him.
All at once he follows her,
    as an ox goes to the slaughter,
or as a stag is caught fast
    till an arrow pierces its liver;
as a bird rushes into a snare;
    he does not know that it will cost him his life.

And now, O sons, listen to me,
    and be attentive to the words of my mouth.
Let not your heart turn aside to her ways;
    do not stray into her paths,
for many a victim has she laid low,
    and all her slain are a mighty throng.

Her house is the way to Sheol,
   going down to the chambers of death.

(Prov. 7:6–27)

Daughter, listen closely. This is the part of the story that changes everything. Out of the corner of my eye, I can see that simple boy. An orange sky warms the deserted streets with the final glow of safe light. He strolls to the edge of the park, just outside my kitchen window. Not noticing anything out of the ordinary, my attention turns back to a half-witty book and my afternoon tea. But after a few sentences more, he turns. Instead of flowing right out my window view, his steps cut left and he doubles back. *Strange*, I think. *Where is he going?* Curious, I begin to watch the wandering traveler. Not many are out at this time in the afternoon, so his lonely wandering catches my interest. Out of my window, I see him. Slowly and casually. He turns. He sits.

He doesn't seem like he is going anywhere in particular. He doesn't seem like he has any schedule to keep. He just walks along, turns around, and aimlessly wanders. His young eyes smile, his happy face is quite content. He is not the least concerned that the bright-orange clouds quickly fade into a deeper shadow of purple.

Lights along the street pop on as evening descends. The little pins of light stand at attention in good order, guarding the perimeter of the quiet park grass—that is, until you reach the end of the street, where the corner sharply turns into the trees. A crooked gray streetlamp slouches at that terrible corner of the street where evil dwells.

The young man continues his journey, wandering along the dark paths, kicking a stone here and there, leaning briefly, putting his hands in his pockets, spinning unpredictably to his new destination. As I watch, he moves closer and closer to that crooked streetlight. Not because he is curious, necessarily, nor because the light is blurry and softer, but simply because he has no other destination, as far as I can tell.

If I could yell to him, if he could hear me through the second-story apartment window, across the street at the other end of the park, I would tell him to turn around. All of the children know to stay away from that dark and dangerous corner. It is the place from where the young and foolish do not return. But my voice is too far away. My counsel is too late to have been heard. He is walking right into the trap. I can only sit and watch from afar.

And then I see her. A wicked woman struts out to meet him. Her crooked smile is deceiving. Her voice is smooth. She looks and sounds too good to be true, but her ways are evil. She calls to the boy to follow her inside the house. Her corrupt hand reaches out for his.

The poor foolish boy! He should have known better. Once she has him in her sight, he is captured. She says all the right things. She cleans up to look so nice. What young man wouldn't be trapped by her smile?

But I know that if any boy enters her house, he will never come out alive. It happens every time without fail. The boy is never strong enough to fight her evil. Prepared or not, she overtakes every good thing about him. Her wickedness is so overpowering, he doesn't even have a chance. If he walks inside, the boy will be lost forever, and he will never see it coming.

Listening from afar, I suddenly recognize this tragic woman. Her words sound just like the tricky lies that came from the serpent in the garden. Sneaky, calm words that conjure up doubt pour from her lips. Once again, a poor creature did the bidding of Satan to trick God's people.

Do you see, daughter? The league of sneaky snake and wicked woman still attack the young. The Evil One lies and seduces by his slaves to fight against the Almighty God. By Satan's command, they lead all down the path of distrust and destruction. Deep into darkness Adam and Eve fell with every bite of disobedience. Darker than the valley of death, our foolish young man is swallowed by the path he now takes.

I look out the window. There is no movement from the house across the street. I know what happened. The boy is gone. He was lost on the path of darkness. He was overcome at the evil house on the end of the street.

My gaze becomes sleepy. Frustrated tears dried three days ago, yet I couldn't look away from that hopeless house. How many more will it swallow? When will the next foolish boy wander along, only to struggle for his last breath? Who can stand up to that terrible, crafty, evil woman?

Early in the pale-gray morning hour, I suddenly see a light flicker in the window at the crooked corner. A soft and clear white fire pierces the morning mist. A candle seems to be rekindled from the deadly quiet shadows. I can barely make out the figure of . . . could it be? The boy? I am almost sure of it, squinting, moving closer to see. It is the likeness of that foolish youth who wandered into the woman's house. But there is a commanding pride now shining from this triumphant boy's face. He is not dead after all—he is alive!

After three long days, the boy bursts from the treacherous tomb. He walks right out of the front door. The first yellow light of dawn shines on his satisfied smile. His clothes even seem to radiate with victory. I watch him fill his lungs with the sweet breath of a new day. By this time, the shabby little gray light at the end of the street is swallowed by the rays of the dawning sun. All the other streetlights bow to this bright and awesome morning. And the boy steps forward, down the right path.

My daughter, what I just witnessed was the incredible journey of a boy who finally smashed the curse of the Evil One. He walked into her house of death willingly. He knew the evil in her heart. He knew her wickedness would kill him. But this Boy still walked inside. She tried to pull him away from the good and faithful path, but ultimately, she was not strong enough. He was no ordinary man. He knew no sin. He was the Son of the Most High God. He was the Word of God Himself.

This Boy is the One promised to Adam and Eve back in the Garden of Eden. We were told that the evil serpent would bite His heel, but He would not die. No, this Boy would rise up and crush the head of the Evil One. Now He has done this, and there is nothing more to fear! The Boy won! He never believed her lies. Even though we saw Him walk into the dreadfully dark house of death, even though we thought He was lost forever, even though we cried as He took her foolish path, this Boy turned everything around. The Evil One has been silenced, and he has no more power to destroy.

Of course, now you recognize your story. Jesus Christ walked among the footsteps of a simple people. Jesus stepped innocently into the house of the Evil One, not because He was tricked, but rather because He knew this was what must be done to save the foolish ones. He was there to pay for the sin of the world, to make this creation "good" again. Since Jesus never sinned, He gave His perfect life as a covering for all. The Father was well pleased with His Son who did no wrong, who walked in the way of Wisdom, who would give His righteous crown to an undeserving people.

But something beyond wonder happens next. Just when I thought it was simply amazing that this young man came back to life and turned back the curse of death, there is even another chapter to our story.

The boy walks out of the silent tomb in that quiet morning hour and seems to stall in the middle of the front yard of that terrible little house. Slowly, he turns back to gaze at the door from which he came. His right hand raises as if to point back to the passage through death. A smile spreads across his shining face. His eyes widen. And something rustles behind the dark threshold.

White lace flutters from the doorframe. Under the gleaming streams of fabric emerges a slender, soft foot. Delicate fingers lay hold of the rotten gray house. She glides halfway outside. A whisper of wind tosses a golden curl behind her creamy-white shoulder. A magnificent woman returns this boy's loving smile. Stretching her toes, she dances toward his outstretched arm. He gently catches her, cradles her in an embrace, and effortlessly carries her away from that house.

The evil woman is gone, but a new and beautiful creature stands in her place. The boy brings out a restored woman, a beautiful bride, a new life. When he walks away from his tomb, he does not go alone; he waits for his lovely wife to share eternal life.

And so it is with our story, my daughter. Jesus did not rise from the dead for Himself; He paid the death toll so that His bride, God's people, would follow Him to everlasting life. Jesus exchanged His pure heart for our black ones, stained by sin. He exchanged our filthy rags for His splendor of righteousness. We are restored beauties by the blood of Christ. We are welcomed at the great wedding feast because Jesus dressed us in His garments. We are the holy people of God because Jesus washed us whiter than snow.

Jesus said that He was the bridegroom for the people of God, and our hearts swelled with hope—He has finally come!

But no one imagined this kind of wedding. No one ever thought that His blessed bride would step out of a deadly, dark cave. No one expected that such a sinner would be cleansed by His death on a cross. No one predicted that He could give such a gift of life to a girl.

You, daughter, are Christ's beautiful bride. But you are walking here not because you are so strong and amazing;

you walk because He cleared the path. He moves your legs, one by one, in His footsteps. He takes your shame when He calls you His own. He covers you in His white victory robe—baptized, chosen, and clean. You walk in the wisdom of this story on account of this Boy. From the Garden of Eden to the house on the corner, God has been looking forward to the day that you will step into a new life. You have been restored to the beauty and wonder of God's creation. You are shining with the life of Christ. By no merit of your own, you are perfect. This is your story.

Chapter 6

Look in the mirror, my daughter. What do you see? Can you see the beautiful girl that God created you to be? Do you see the white robe of righteousness that Christ put on you? Do you see a perfect and blameless life that lives inside of your heart? Probably not. You might see a familiar face that you remember looking back at you on both happy days and sad days, but she looks pretty normal. Maybe she doesn't even look all that special. You might wonder, *How could this girl in the mirror be the amazing bride that Christ loves?*

Little girl, we all ask that question. I remember pulling a blue brush through my elementary-school hair, looking at the reflection of an ordinary girl. She just stared back at me, pondering the same thing. No matter how young or old, each woman looks deep into her own eyes and wonders, *Am I that special? How do I really know He did this for me?*

Some will have you believe a story from your heart. They will counsel you to search your feelings and your passions to know the truth. They will tell you to quietly meditate and be mindful in the "now" to experience the new life. But they are wrong—this is the same deception the serpent used in the garden to pull Eve away from God's real promises—woman's real identity. This evil voice says, "Did God really say . . . ?" The terrible liar whispers, "It's not that easy." The ugly snake hisses, "You are not worth it—just live for today."

No, my daughter. You are God's own child. You are baptized into Christ! It is not because of how you look. It is not because of how you feel. It has nothing to do with your wildly searching heart. You are the special bride of Christ because He alone chose you.

He finds you cowering in the bushes when you have done wrong. He finds you wandering through the dark valleys of sadness. He finds you screaming as a helpless baby or an ashamed adult, but He still washes you clean and makes you His own. Water sprinkled on your little head, words filling your little ears, a cross upon your forehead and upon your heart. That simple heavenly flood marks you as a beloved child—now and forever.

Inhale the fresh summer air and just remember the wonderful gifts given in the Garden of Eden. Everything was new and beautiful. It's no surprise God created His creatures to love and listen. He was the head; His creatures submitted. God provided everything for His man and woman—food, companionship, rest, life, and love. The people had an identity created for them: God's children.

Remember the story of the dusty desert, where the chosen people, Israel, had a long history experiencing God's love. He selected the small and insignificant people in order to make them great. God supplied everything for His nation; food in the wilderness, water in the desert, leadership through seas and darkness, salvation from slavery. He asked only one thing in return: "You shall have no other Gods." Even though they failed, God made them into His beloved children.

Remember when a tiny baby, who was the Light of the World, cried out into the night. He was born in a manger, lowering Himself into the dirt. This frail, stinky child would grow to do everything that Almighty God asked of Him.

He taught the Father's Word, He remained faithful, helpful, and in submission. Even when Jesus feared that His road was too hard, He still continued down the path in loving silence. God was pleased with every perfect action of His beloved child.

Remember your story; remember watching our Hero stroll down a dark, forbidden street. He walked through the door of certain death. He entered the house of evil because of love. He lowered Himself all the way into the grave, submitting to death for the life of His bride. His submission was for you. And He rose from the dead so that you will live forever with Him.

You know this is true because this is the promise of Jesus, the Son of God.

> Jesus answered, "Truly, truly, I say to you, unless one is born of water and the Spirit, he cannot enter the kingdom of God." (John 3:5 ESV)

You have entered into the kingdom of God! So when Satan and despair and sadness and death come calling, you know what to say to them, my daughter. When your story is challenged by a silly world or questioned by your unsure heart, you still know who you are. You are born of water and spirit! You are baptized into Christ! You are chosen by God! You are the beautiful bride of the Savior!

And so it's not really a question of what to do now. You will just do what God created you to do from the very beginning. No checklist or report card. Who you are doesn't depend on you and your choices. You are free again to live in a good relationship with your Creator. And guess what? Right in the middle of this story, you will find that you love what God loves. You will notice that His good is your good. You will recognize what a blessing it is to be His beloved creation, and you will desire it more and more.

Daughter, when we see who God made us to be, we see glimpses of our created beauty. When a man guards and provides for his family like he was created to do, we get a taste of the peace God promised. When a woman sets her own desires aside and helps her husband as she was made to do, we recognized the beauty of God's restored creation. When a child listens and obeys his parents, we hear echoes of praise from the proud Almighty Father reconciled to His people once again.

We are masks of God in each other's lives. He works through our words and actions, hidden behind ordinary voices and fingers. The God of everything cares for you so much that He acts in the filthy dust of our messy lives. We know He is here with every good and gracious father. We feel His care with every quiet and hopeful mother. We believe His promise of new life with every baptism. We hear, feel, taste, smell, and even see the hand of God in a blurry picture of paradise.

And this is your amazing story. You have been given a new life—no matter what the mirror looks like today, no matter what your feelings tell you about tomorrow. You are baptized into Christ. You are a beautiful bride that will forever live in paradise. This is your story.

Chapter 7

The long dusty road leads Sarah to Gerar. The country is unfamiliar, and she has no idea what to expect from this town she now approaches. With every step closer to the little village, she strains her ears to listen for strange men approaching. Her stomach twists in fear for what this place would do to Sarah and her husband, Abraham.

Sarah, our sister in faith, believes this story despite her own hard circumstances. Her husband, Abraham, is a gift. He protects her, he loves her, he is the hands and mouth of the hidden God for her. And yes, Abraham is a sinner. There are times when Sarah is afraid. There are times when she is confused and mad. There are times when she thinks it is just too hard to continue, but she hopes in God. She looks at her husband and treats him as the mask of God.

Earlier in their journey together, Sarah was told that she would bear a child. Both she and her husband are very old. Yet God keeps His promise to her, despite the dismal and unlikely circumstances. Sarah trusts in God's good and gracious gifts. She believes Abraham's words and God's promises. She expects Him to care for her, even when she is unsure of her future. She hopes in God and beautifully reflects the woman that God created in the garden.

Years later, a much younger girl is surprised by unfortunate circumstances. Unmarried, promised to another, she discovers she is pregnant. How humiliating it is when her friends whisper. How heartbreaking it is when she has to leave her home, dishonored. But the mother of our Lord, Mary, hopes in God. She believes this story and says, "I am a servant of the Lord; let it be to me according to your word" (Luke 1:38).

Sadly, our world today would tell Sarah and Mary that they were wrong. It would counsel these girls to seek their own happiness. It would chastise them for not speaking their minds. It would empower them to fight against the injustices they experienced. But Sarah and Mary hoped in God. They held tightly to the ancient story that Wisdom revealed to them. Because they trusted their sure identities before God, they could love even in the midst of unhappy circumstances.

However, you, daughter—you are in the most hopeful stage of life right now. Paths unknown, friends to come, a husband, children, years of memories looking forward into the future. An imagination full of the happy dreams to come. Your choices now will set a path for the rest of your life. Your story will help guide you on the path that women of God have been walking for centuries. Your beloved Christ has freed you from the lies of the devil, the world, and your own sinful heart.

But even if you make the best choices, your own path will be hard. Death still saddens, pain still stings, uncontrollable unknowable events still haunt the walk of a Christian woman. You will cry, lose loved ones, regret, and fall down. Those who are meant to care for and love you will fail, disappoint you, sin against you, and fall down. Together we live in a broken world. Together we live with selfish hearts. Together we live with the voice of the Deceiver—wanting us to turn away from the precious Word of God.

What we realize quickly is that hardship will meet us more often than not in this lifetime. Most of us have never even seen a relationship that loves like this: a man who leads patiently and justly, a woman who submits happily and quietly. We long to be in this story, the one that works out beautifully as God intended. We want to be the happy creations of a God who loves them. We seek an unblemished relationship with creatures who walk through this world together. We are almost too afraid to imagine it is true.

> For we know that the whole creation has been groaning together in the pains of childbirth until now. And not only the creation, but we ourselves, who have the firstfruits of the Spirit, groan inwardly as we wait eagerly for adoption as sons, the redemption of our bodies. (Rom. 8:22–23)

It gets even worse. Our visible disappointments are not only in relationships; even the water and the trees cry out to their Creator. All of creation was torn apart by sin. Trees and plants do not produce fruit like they once did. Weeds and dust choke out the life God created for His earth. Water poisons and floods communities. It hides in drought and kills the people that God created. Our bodies were crafted to be fed by the gifts of creation: food and water. Yet these days, even creation groans and dies alongside us.

It's not right! Men hurt women. Trees wilt and die. Women yearn to be alone. This world hates men protecting daughters, wives, and widows. Trusting hearts are abandoned by those whom were created to love. This culture entices women to get degrees and jobs to measure their worth. The righteous suffer, fall away, and die. These are perversions of God's good creation. And we live right in the middle of it. But we still hope in the story that we can only hear with our ears.

You are created purposefully. You are created beautifully. You are created to help. You are created to love quietly, gently, submissively, and fearlessly. And you have been given back this amazing identity of a woman. You are the beautiful bride of Christ no matter what! We will continue to watch for everything to be made new and peaceful and fruitful once again. We expect God to show us the work He has finished completely in Christ. We hold on with anticipation.

The ending to our story is yet to come.